The Ekklesia of Christ

Becoming the People of God

Berean Study Series

THE EKKLESIA OF CHRIST
Becoming the People of God
Published by Heritage Christian University Press

Manufactured in the United States of America

Cataloging-in-Publication Data

The Ekklesia of Christ: becoming the people of God /edited by Ed Gallagher
Berean study series
p. cm.
Includes Scripture index.
ISBN 978-17320483-2-4 (pbk.)
1. Church—Biblical teaching—Study and teaching.
I. Gallagher, Edmon L. II. Title. III. Series.
BS680 .E64 2015 262—dc20 2019-933599

Cover design by Brittany McGuire and Brad McKinnon

Contents

THE EKKLESIA OF CHRIST

Introduction

Why the Church?

Ed Gallagher

The church is the hope for the world. This bold assertion may strike many Christian readers as patently false—far from being the hope for the world; the church is everything that is wrong with Christianity. The church represents the institutional nature of Christianity, rules-based religion, and hypocrisy. Give me Jesus without the church! For Jesus is who is the hope for the world. He is the one who provides the perfect example of a life lived in service to God. He is the one who ate with sinners and welcomed prostitutes while chastising the hypocritical Pharisees. He is the one who sacrificed himself on behalf of others, whose blood washes away sin. He is the one who conquered death, who ascended to the right hand of God, who always intercedes on our behalf. He is the one who left behind a community of followers to carry on his mission of turning the world upside down.

Aye, there's the rub. That community of followers that Jesus left behind is the church. If the church is the body of Christ, as Paul says on a number of occasions (e.g., 1 Cor 12:26; Col 1:18), then you cannot have Christ without the church. (That would be like Christ without Christ.) If the church manifests the kingdom of God in the world today, then it continues the mission of the one who came announcing that kingdom. If the church is a royal priesthood and a holy nation, as Peter thinks (1 Pet 2:9), then the world needs the church to be what God designed it to be. If God has planned the church from all eternity (Eph 1:4) and intended the church to reveal his "manifold wisdom" to "the rulers and authorities in the heavenly places" (Eph 3:10), then what does that mean for the importance of the church? The community Christ left behind shares his vocation of being a light to the nations (Isa 49:6; Matt 5:14) and bringing salvation to the ends of the earth (Matt 28:19). The church is the hope for the world.

The importance of the church in God's scheme of redemption becomes clear when studying Paul's interpretation of scripture. He continually interprets the Old Testament scriptures as finding their fulfillment in the communities that he is forming throughout Europe and Asia. When the law of Moses forbids muzzling a threshing ox (Deut 25:4), Paul insists that this commandment was written “altogether for our sake” (1 Cor 9:9–10). The story of Israel’s sin with the golden calf (Exod 32) was “written for our instruction” (1 Cor 10:11; cf. Rom 15:4). Just as Christ fulfills the promise to Abraham of a seed (Gal 3:16; cf. Gen 22:18), so we who are in Christ are also Abraham’s seed (Gal 3:29). One scholar has described this interpretive strategy as Paul’s “ecclesiocentric hermeneutic,” a hermeneutic centered on the church (ecclesia).[1] Paul sees much of the Bible as leading up to and foreshadowing the church.

Terminology

The Greek word *ekklēsia* signifies the assembly of believers, and many languages have taken their word for “church” from this word (cf. Latin *ecclesia*, French *église*, Spanish *iglesia*). The English language is different in this regard: the English word “church” derives not from *ekklēsia* but from a different Greek word, *kuriakon*, an adjectival form of *kurios*, meaning “lord” (a common description of Jesus or God in Greek). The adjective *kuriakos* appears a couple of times in the New Testament, once to describe the “lordly” supper (1 Cor 11:20), and another time to describe the “lordly” day (Rev 1:10). In the fourth century, the adjective could signify the “lordly” house, that is, the church building,

1. See Richard B. Hays, *Echoes of Scripture in the Letters of Paul* (New Haven: Yale University Press, 1989).

as in the following example from the early church historian Eusebius: "[The Roman Emperor Maximinus II] now allows [Christians] both to observe their form of worship and to build church buildings [*kuriaka*, plural of *kuriakon*]."[2]

Here the word *kuriakon* simply means "church building." When the German tribes heard this word used for church buildings, they adopted it and applied it more broadly not only to the building but also to the institution, or the people who met in the building. The Germans bequeathed this word to the English, who made their own adjustments to the spelling and pronunciation, producing our word "church." But this word, "church," is now used as a translation of the New Testament word *ekklēsia*.

In the New Testament, the word *ekklēsia* appears 114 times, almost always referring to a Christian congregation or assembly. It does not have this meaning every time, such as in Acts 19:40, where it refers to an "assembly" of a pagan mob. The word also appears in the Greek Old Testament—the Septuagint, commonly abbreviated LXX—one hundred times, usually in reference to the assembly of Israel. For an example, see

2. Eusebius, *Ecclesiastical History* 9.10.12.

Deuteronomy 31:30.[3] A similar Greek term, *synagōgē*, appears even more often in the LXX, a total of 221 times (e.g., Lev. 8:3). The two terms both mean "assembly" or "congregation," but by the first century it appears that the second of these terms, *synagōgē*, had taken on the meaning of a meeting place of Jews for Sabbath worship. Likely, it was this use of *synagōgē* that led the Jewish followers of the resurrected Messiah to avoid the term for their gatherings and prefer the other term that was prominent in the Greek version of Israel's scriptures, *ekklēsia*.[4]

Significance

The term "church" appears only three times in the Gospels, each time on the lips of Jesus in the Gospel of Matthew. This simple statistic makes it immediately clear that Jesus did not often speak about the church in those terms. Rather, he spoke of the kingdom of God, a phrase that appears 126 times in the Gospels (including related terminology, such as "kingdom of heaven"). But Jesus certainly did intend to form a community of believers who would embody his teachings and

3. The Old Testament was originally composed in Hebrew. It was translated into Greek beginning in the third century BC. This Greek translation, the Septuagint, was often quoted in the New Testament and became the Old Testament for the early Greek-speaking Christians. It is still the Old Testament for the Greek Orthodox Church.

4. See Paul Trebilco, *Self-designations and Group Identity in the New Testament* (Cambridge: Cambridge University Press, 2012), 164–207.

represent him to the world after his departure. The concept of the church appears more frequently in Jesus' discourses than a simple count of the appearances of the term would indicate.

The two passages in which Jesus uses the term *ekklēsia* shed important light on the nature of the community envisioned by Jesus.[5] The first passage is the famous scene near Caesarea Philippi when Peter first confesses that Jesus is the Christ (Matt 16:13–28). In response to this confession, Jesus says, in part, "I also say to you that you are Peter, and upon this rock I will build My church; and the gates of Hades will not overpower it" (v. 18). This verse has generated a great deal of discussion, especially in terms of the relationship between Peter and the rock.[6] Without entering deeply into the discussion, I would simply point out that Peter's confession may be the rock upon which the church is built, but even if the rock is intended to be Peter himself, the meaning would not diverge far from

5. It is unlikely that Jesus used the Greek word *ekklēsia* in his teaching. Jesus likely spoke Aramaic, and he probably used a corresponding Hebrew or Aramaic term, such as Hebrew *qahal* (Aramaic: *qehēla*), which underlies each of the appearances of *ekklēsia* in the LXX.

6. See, for instance, Joseph A. Burgess, *A History of the Exegesis of Matthew 16:17–19 from 1781 to 1965* (Ann Arbor: Edwards Brothers, 1976). See also Jack P. Lewis, "'The Gates of Hell Shall Not Prevail Against It' (Matt 16:18): A Study of the History of Interpretation," *Journal of the Evangelical Theological Society* 38 (1995): 349–67.

Paul's assertion that the apostles and prophets form the foundation of the church (Eph 2:20).

It is important to recognize two aspects of Jesus' use of the word "church" here. First, the word means "community" or "assembly." It is often said that "church" means the "called-out," but this is incorrect. While the word *ekklēsia* is formed by a prefix meaning "out" (*ek*-), and a lexeme meaning "called" (*klēsia*; cf. the verb *kaleō*), the compound term *ekklēsia* did not bear this significance, certainly not in first-century Greek. While Christians should be in some important ways separate from the world, we do not derive this teaching from the etymology of the word for "church." Rather, *ekklēsia* means "community," and this, in itself, is of vast significance for the nature of the Christian life. Jesus did not envision individual Christian free agents, concerned merely with their own salvation and their personal relationship with God. In this passage, it is not the individual Christian who would carry on Christ's mission in the world. Jesus established a community, a group of believers who would work together, who would care for one another, who would jointly represent Christ. Jesus himself gives the lie to the idea that one can have Christ without the church.

Second, the term *ekklēsia* connects the community established by Jesus with the community of Israel. One who reads the English Bible, beginning with Genesis, would not encounter the word "church" until Matthew

16:18, and thus might conclude that Jesus was introducing a brand-new concept. But the disciples do not question Jesus about what he means by this word "church." They knew precisely what an *ekklēsia* was because the term appeared frequently in their Scriptures in reference to the community of Israel. Jesus had come to form a renewed Israel, in line with Old Testament prophecies (e.g., Ezek 37:15–28; Jer 31:31). The new *ekklēsia* established by Jesus would be continuous with the people of God from the calling of Abraham forward.

The next time Jesus uses the word "church," he is addressing a procedure for dealing with a "brother" who sins (Matt 18:15–17). If this brother does not repent based on a personal conversation or, failing that, an intervention with a couple other believers, then the matter should come before the community (the church), and the community should attempt to persuade this brother. This text highlights the responsibility that the community bears for one another. This is no loose organization to which we can pay our annual dues and participate in if we choose. No, confessing Christ as Lord entails membership in a committed Christian community with the responsibility of helping other members of the community to maintain their faithfulness to Christ, and to accept their intervention on our behalf. Jesus intimated that his group of followers was a new type of family (Mark 3:31–35), and the term "brothers (and sisters)" is the most common designation in Paul's letters for Christians. The community of Christ is to be as committed to one another as a family. Almost always in Paul's letters (Ephesians and Colossians are exceptions), the term *ekklēsia* refers not vaguely to the church universal but concretely to the local congregation. This is where the rubber meets the road. The call of Jesus is a call to an actual assembly of flesh-and-blood people, with all their sins, annoyances, and folly, to be sure, but also with all their love, sacrifice, and goodwill. Whether we like it or not, Jesus has established his church, and he expects us to demonstrate a commitment to it as part of what it means to be committed to him.

Our Hope

If we want to understand our Lord better and what he expects of his followers, then we need to understand what Scripture teaches about the church. We hope that this series of studies will bless you as you seek to be salt and light to your community. We hope that it will invigorate you with the exhilarating message of the kingdom of God. We hope that it will empower you to fulfill the mission that God has entrusted to his church. We hope it will encourage your commitment to the community of believers to which God has added you (cf. Acts 2:47). Read these studies with other Christians. Look up the scripture references together. Grow in your faith together with the family of God.

Discussion Questions

1. Can you be a faithful Christian without being a part of a local congregation? How would Jesus or Paul respond to this question?

2. How does the meaning of the term "church" or *ekklēsia* contribute to our identity as the people of God?

3. What responsibility does the church have for on another?

4. What responsibility does the church have for the world?

1

The Kingdom of God

Ed Gallagher

Churches of Christ have long emphasized the close relationship between the kingdom of God and the church. Such an emphasis is entirely appropriate since the New Testament envisions the church and the kingdom in extremely similar terms.[1] Perhaps we have emphasized it a little too strongly, for Scripture does not present the kingdom of God as completely identical to the church; they are different concepts.[2] And yet, the church is the current earthly manifestation of the

1. See Scot McKnight, *Kingdom Conspiracy: Returning to the Radical Mission of the Local Church* (Grand Rapids: Brazos, 2014), who largely seeks to affirm the close relationship between church and kingdom.

2. See Luke 12:32, where the community of Jesus (later to be called the church) would receive the kingdom, and so cannot be identical to it. The only passage that applies the label "kingdom" directly to the church is Rev 1:6.

kingdom of God, the people who exhibit God's reign in the world now, who live within the kingdom even as they await its full revelation. If you are looking for evidence of God's kingdom today, the place to look is the church. Biblical teaching about the kingdom of God contributes to a better appreciation of the church's role within God's plan of salvation.

The first words out of the mouth of Jesus in the Gospel of Mark consist of an announcement that the kingdom of God would soon commence (Mark 1:15). Such an announcement would have been received by Jesus' contemporaries with, perhaps, a mix of anticipation (the oppressed crowds), trepidation (the political leaders), and disbelief (nearly everyone). For hundreds of years, Judah had been dominated by foreign powers, from the Assyrians, to the Babylonians, to the Persians, Greeks, and now the Romans. While some first-century Jews no doubt longed for the time when God would establish his kingdom, others had probably long since ceased holding their breath.

The announcement by Jesus signaled the impending fulfillment of a variety of Old Testament promises. To be sure, God has always been king, and in that sense, he has had a kingdom.[3] But the prophets had in varying ways envisioned a time when God would reign as king more fully and visibly than he currently did. The

3. For OT passages mentioning the kingship of God, see Psa 47:2; 93:1; 95:3; 97:1; 98:6; 99:1; cf. 1 Sam 8:7.

pivotal promise appears in 2 Samuel 7. God would establish David's dynasty, guaranteeing that one of his descendants would always reign over Israel (2 Sam 7:12–16). Through this "son of David," God would reign, for the son of David would also be the "son of God" (2 Sam 7:14).

It quickly became apparent that the immediate descendants of David in no way lived up to the great promise of 2 Samuel 7. Though Solomon accomplished some great things (1 Kgs 3–10), he also oppressed the people (1 Kgs 12:4), promoted idolatry (1 Kgs 11:1–8), and indirectly caused the division of the kingdom into two separate nations (Judah and Israel) following his death (1 Kgs 12:1–15). And most of the other kings of Judah and Israel weren't even that good. Even while the Davidic dynasty was going strong, Isaiah longed for a time when "a shoot will spring from the stem of Jesse" (Isa 11:1). This new king from David's line—Jesse was David's father (1 Sam 16:1)—would bear the divine Spirit and would judge the people with righteousness, lifting up the poor and slaying the wicked (Isa 11:2–5). In his days, there would be universal peace, even between animals and men, so much so that children need have no fear of poisonous snakes (Isa 11:6–9). The reign of this king would usher in a time of paradise, and God would reign through him.

Other prophets present their own visions of what it would look like when God reigns, when he establishes his kingdom. Ezekiel, a priest, imagines an enormous temple (chs. 40–48) from which flows a great river nourishing life-giving trees (Ezek 47:1–12) and, most importantly, God himself inhabits this temple (Ezek 43:5). God will live among his people. Micah imagines God as a shepherd who would "assemble the lame and gather the outcasts" to be his kingdom (Mic 4:6–8). Sometimes in these visions of God's kingdom, the Gentile nations flock to Zion to learn God's will and join in worshipping him (cf. Mic 4:1–3; Isa 2:2–4; cf. Isa 56:1–8; 60). Often it was imagined that twelve tribes of Israel would be regathered under one king, the new David (Jer 23:5–6; Ezek 37:15–28).

And so, though some people may have doubted the sanity of Jesus, no one could doubt his meaning when he declared that the time had finally arrived when God would begin to reign. Indeed, Jesus was the one through whom God would inaugurate his kingdom; he was the messiah, as Peter and the apostles finally realized (Mark 8:29). When he cast out demons, the kingdom had come near (Luke 11:20). When he healed people of their diseases, he engaged in battle with the evil forces arrayed against God (Luke 13:16). He fought with Satan in the wilderness, and he overcame (Matt 4:1–11). His twelve chosen disciples (Mark 3:13–19) represented the regathered tribes of Israel (cf. Luke 22:30), just as he also attracted followers from roughly the geography of David's kingdom (Matt 4:23–25). He was the one, as Isaiah prophesied, on whom the spirit rested (Luke 4:16–21). He was the son of David whose throne would be established forever (Matt 1:1).

But he was different than what had been anticipated, and he spoke of a different kind of kingdom than what was expected. Not only was he David's son, but he was David's lord (Matt 22:41–46). In the kingdom preached by Jesus, blessings were pronounced on the poor in spirit, the merciful, the peacemakers (Matt 5:3–12). Jesus' kingdom was one that welcomed sinners (Mark 2:15–16; Luke 7:36–50) and prostitutes (Matt 21:31–32) and—worse yet—Gentiles (cf. Isa 2:2–4) while the most religious individuals were threatened with exclusion (Matt 8:11–12). This king, this expected one, who healed the sick and opened the eyes of the blind and preached the gospel to the poor (Matt 11:2–6), unexpectedly refused to proclaim himself king openly (John 6:15; cf. Mark 1:24, 44; 3:11–12) and did not take up arms against Israel's enemy, Rome (Matt 26:52). Indeed, just the opposite: he allowed himself to be mocked, tortured, and crucified by Rome. Certainly an odd type of king.

Yet the crucifixion was central to Jesus' notion of the kingdom. It was, after all, at the moment of crucifixion when Jesus received his royal crown (Mark 15:17) and hung under a sign proclaiming him king (Mark 15:26). He had warned his disciples that this was going to happen (Mark 8:31; 9:31; 10:33–34) and that they themselves would have to do similarly (Mark 8:34). In Jesus' kingdom, the first would be last (Mark 10:31) and the leaders would be servants (Mark 10:42–45; John 13:1–10).

The citizens of Jesus' kingdom would be characterized by self-sacrifice (Matt 25:31–46), love (Matt 22:34–40), and commitment to one another (Matt 18:15–18). They would live by an elevated ethic, beyond normal interpretations of Moses' law (Matt 5:17–48). Not just adultery, but even lust was prohibited. Not just murder, but even hate was forbidden. Loving neighbors was fine, but citizens of this new kingdom would love their enemies. They would go the extra mile and turn the other cheek. They would do their righteous deeds to be noticed not by men but by God (Matt 6:1–18). They would trust God to provide their daily needs as they sought above all his kingdom (Matt 6:25–34). They would refuse to judge others but would walk the strait and narrow path (Matt 7:1–14). By living out the teachings of Jesus, they would prove themselves worthy of entering the kingdom of heaven (Matt 7:21).[4]

When "all authority in heaven and on earth" has been given to Jesus following his suffering and

4. On Matthew's peculiar use of the term "kingdom of heaven" rather than "kingdom of God," as in the other Gospels, see Jonathan T. Pennington, *Heaven and Earth in the Gospel of Matthew* (Leiden: Brill, 2007; Grand Rapids: Baker, 2009).

resurrection (Matt 28:18)—that is, following his victory over death and the evil powers (Col 2:15; Heb 2:14–15)—clearly what Jesus has been announcing throughout his ministry has now come to pass: he is king; the kingdom of God has begun. If the kingdom does not appear as we might have guessed from the prophetic visions, Jesus himself had cautioned us: only those who are born again can see the kingdom of God (John 3:3). Only renewed eyes of faith can discern the reign of God in the small group of Jews who stubbornly insist that someone crucified as a traitor had truly been and truly is the Messiah, the king in a newly established kingdom. When people accept this message and obey the teachings of Jesus the Messiah (Christ), God transfers them out of the kingdom of darkness and into the kingdom of his dear son (Col 1:13).

But the kingdom of God is not yet fully revealed. Jesus inaugurated it but has not yet brought it to completion. We still pray for God's kingdom to come (Matt 6:10) because we long for the time when all creation will bow before Jesus and acclaim him lord (Phil 2:9–11; Rev 5:13). The church is an outpost of the kingdom of God now, a community already living under the rule of God in accordance with the ethic Jesus established, looking forward to inheriting the kingdom (Rom 8:17; cf. 1 Cor 6:9; 15:50) at the consummation of all things.

More than a century ago, Alfred Loisy wrote, "Jesus announced the kingdom, and it is the church that came."[5] The church may seem a disappointment in comparison with the expectations created by Jesus' kingdom announcement. Perhaps such disappointment is in part due to the failure of Christians to embody the kingdom message of Jesus. The church ought to find its identity in "Jesus' vision of the kingdom of God and its instantiation in a community of disciples, which already manifests, in the character of its life, the nature of God's coming universal rule."[6] Or, as Paul would have it, "the rule of God takes effect in the present in the fruit of the Spirit and in the gifts of the Spirit."[7] All too often in churches of Christ, it seems, we have equated the kingdom of God with the church—often in a battle against premillennialism—for the purpose of taming the kingdom, bringing it down to the normal, everyday level of the church. It would be more in keeping with Jesus' teaching to magnify the church as the present manifestation of God's kingdom, and therein find our mission and calling.

5. Alfred Loisy, *L'Évangile et l'Église* (3d ed.; Bellevue: Chez l'auteur, 1904), 155 : "Jésus annonçait le royaume, et c'est l'Église qui est venue."

6. Richard Bauckham, "Kingdom and Church According to Jesus and Paul," *Horizons in Biblical Theology* 18.1 (1996): 1–26, at 14.

7. Bauckham, "Kingdom and Church," 16.

Questions for Discussion

1. How is the church related to the kingdom of God?

2. Is the kingdom of God present or future?

3. How did the prophets imagine the kingdom of God? Where do these visions find their fulfillment?

4. Does the relationship between the church and the kingdom of God help to give purpose to our lives as Christians?

2

The Israel of God

Nathan Daily

Even though the phrase "Israel of God" occurs only one time in the Bible (Gal 6:16),[1] it stands alongside several images of the church that echo the content of the Hebrew Scriptures: "a chosen race," "a holy nation" (1 Pet 2:9), "twelve tribes" (Matt 19:28; Jas 1:1; Rev 7), "remnant" (Rom 11:5), and "Abraham's offspring" (Rom 4:16).[2] Each of these help provide definition for how a community can imagine what it means to be known as the people of God.

1. Cf. Eph 2:12; Heb 8:8–13; Rev 2:14; Matt 15:24; Acts 5:31; Luke 2:32.

2. Paul S. Minear, *Images of the Church in the New Testament*, NTL (Louisville: Westminster, 1960; repr., 2004), 66–84.

Whereas some might speak of a "new" or "spiritual" Israel, this language is not found in the Bible.[3] In fact, positing one Israel against another can detract from the continuity regarding the nature of God's people that Paul is attempting to build through his use of the imagery in the Letter to the Galatians. Ultimately, Paul's use of the phrase "Israel of God" encourages Christians to hear the entirety of the story of God and God's people. After connecting the promises of God in the Hebrew Scriptures with the acts of God through the life and death of Jesus, Paul's reference to Christians as the "Israel of God" becomes a significant image upon which Christians can create identity as they imagine both the benefits and obligations of inclusion within the people of God.

The Story of Israel

Before attempting to understand Paul's reference to the Israel of God in Gal 6:16, it is necessary to recall the story of Israel. In the broadest of strokes, the narrative portions of the Hebrew Scriptures (Gen–Esther) can be read thematically as a story from creation (Gen 1–11), to the promises to Abraham, Sarah, and their children (Gen 12–50), to salvation from Egypt (Exod–Deut), to life in the Promised Land (Josh–1 Kgs 11), to the crises of divided kingdom and exile (1 Kgs 12–2 Kgs), and toward hope of restoration (1 Chr–Esth).

3. See the theologically misleading interpretation of Gal 6:16 in the New Living Translation.

The poems (Job–Song) and prophets (Isa–Mal) of the Hebrew Scriptures provide an abundance of voices from the people of God throughout the history of Israel that express the varied experiences of life during these times as well as reactions to the joys, tragedies, and hopes narrated within the story.

Throughout time, God's people have read, re-read, and discussed these texts not only to understand what happened in the past, but also in order to imagine how they, as readers, might create identity in the present. God's people believe that true living occurs when a community attempts to understand, question, and discuss the depictions of God and humans, the relationships between God and humanity, and the relationships between humans in these texts. Experiencing what life is really about follows connecting to and living in tandem with the story of God and God's people.

Much of the story of Israel[4] can be read through the lens of promise and expectation. In Gen 12:1–3, Abram is singularly selected by God and receives from God a promise. The elements of this promise include land, becoming a great nation, and God's blessing extending beyond Abram's family to all nations. As Genesis

4. Notable exceptions include Job, Ecclesiastes, and Song of Songs. See, Richard Bauckham, "Reading Scripture as a Coherent Story," in *The Art of Reading Scripture* (ed. Ellen F. Davis and Richard B. Hays; Grand Rapids: Eerdmans, 2003), 38–53.

progresses, the elderly, childless, and landless Abram and Sarai (Gen 12:4; 16:16; 17:1, 17; 18:11–12; 21:2,7) leave as commanded (Gen 12:1) but are met with a series of challenges (e.g., Gen 12:10–20; 20:1–18; 22:1–19) that threaten the promise. Even as Abram and Sarai remain childless, God continues to reassert the promise of land and offspring (Gen 13:14–17; 15; 17; 21; 22:15–18) even though much of the promise may remain only partially fulfilled for many years (Gen 15:13–21). Following the tensest moment in the narrative, the binding of Isaac (Gen 22:1–19), which places the entirety of the promise in jeopardy, God reasserts the promise upon Abraham and his descendants (Gen 22:16–18).

Remembrance of God's promise to Abraham is highlighted throughout the Torah (Exod 2:24; 3:15; 6:8; Lev 26:42; Deut 1:8; 29:13; etc.)[5] in expectation of entrance into the Promised Land (Deut 31:23; Josh 23:5). Life in the land brings rest and fulfillment of God's promise to Abraham (Josh 21:44; 22:4; 23:1, 15; Jud 2:1). However, the safety of land comes with warning: Israel should not assume that peace equates with independence from need of their God. Obedience remains priority (Josh 23:6–8, 16; 24:14ff.). Ultimately, this threat begins to be realized as the nation divides into

5. On this theme in the Torah see, David J. A. Clines, *The Theme of the Pentateuch* (2d ed.; Library of Hebrew Bible/Old Testament Studies 10; New York: Bloomsbury, 1997).

two kingdoms (1 Kings 12–14; cf. 1 Kings 11:1–2; Josh 24:14ff.). The great nation promised to Abraham (Gen 12:2) and fulfilled before entering the land (Deut 26:5) can no longer be called great. As matters deteriorate, both nations (Northern Israel and Judah) meet a sad end in exile (2 Kgs 17; 2 Kgs 25).

Within this moment of exile, Israel seeks hope in God's promise to Abraham (Isa 41:8; 51:2). The hope is that because of this promise, God will restore Israel to her former glory (Ezek 37:15–28; Isa 49:1–6; cf. Jer 27:22; Jer 30:3; 33:7; Ezek 39:25; Acts 1:8; etc.). Just as Israel never forgets the promise initially articulated to Abraham in Gen 12, the New Testament authors regularly cite God's promise to Abraham as a foundational moment that provides meaning for the whole of the biblical story (Luke 1:46–55; 67–79; Acts 3:13, 25; 7; Rom 4:13; 11:1; Gal 3:6–9, 14–18, 29; etc).

Israel, Jesus, and the Galatians

Paul's familiarity with the story of Israel and his understanding of the importance of God's promise to Abraham for the emergence and sustaining of the people of God provide the foundation for his closing salutation to the Galatian Christians as the Israel of God (6:16). The Letter to the Galatians is a written argument by Paul to address and attempt to correct a crisis in the churches of Galatia.[6] The crisis emerged as Christian teachers or missionaries entered the Galatian churches and taught a different gospel from that of Paul. Specifically, they demanded circumcision for Gentiles who convert to the people of God (Gal 1:6–7; 3.1; 4:17; 5:2–4, 7–12; 6:12–13; cf. Gen 17:10, 14). At the time Paul writes the letter, these missionaries were succeeding in convincing the Galatians that in order to be in the covenant people, heirs of the promise to Abraham, they must uphold the works of the law (4:8–11; cf. 3:10).[7] Paul vehemently disagrees with this proposal (1:6; 3:1). At stake is "who are the people of God" and "upon what condition does one join the people of God." Whereas Paul and the missionaries would agree that it is necessary to be an heir of Abraham in order to be within the people of God, Paul argues that the basis enabling a Gentile to become Abraham's heir is not a Jewish identity marker like circumcision (Gal 2:3–12;

6. On Galatians see, Louis Martyn, *Galatians* (AB 33A; New York: Doubleday, 1997); Richard B. Hays, *NIB* 11:181–348; Frank J. Matera, *Galatians* (SP 9; Collegeville: Liturgical, 1992); James D. G. Dunn, *The Epistle to the Galatians* (BNTC 9; Peabody: Hendrickson, 1993); David A. DeSilva, *An Introduction to the New Testament: Contexts, Methods & Ministry Formation* (Downers Grove: IVP Academic, 2004), 493–526; N. T. Wright, *Galatians and Thessalonians* (Paul for Everyone; Louisville: Westminster, 2002).

7. Hays, 184.

5:2, 6, 11; 6:12, 15; cf. 4:8–11). Rather, the basis for inclusion is the faithfulness of Jesus Christ, i.e., his death.

The importance of Jesus' death on the cross as a cosmos-changing event cannot be underestimated. This death has changed the world from old to new, so that certain seemingly significant categories have now become nonexistent relics of an old world (6:14–15; cf. 5:6; 1:3–5; 1 Cor 7:19). The primary issue of contention in the letter, circumcision, is, in fact, a prime example of the move from the old age to the new age. Therefore, Paul explicitly highlights circumcision one final time at the close of the letter (6:15). One unified church may include uncircumcised Gentile Galatians as well as circumcised Jewish Christians. However, emphasis upon ethnic markers of identity belongs to a world that no longer exists after the death of Jesus (3:23–4:11).[8] These categories no longer matter because when God sets the world right through the death of Jesus (1:1–5; 2:16–21), Gentiles receive the promise God made to Abram in Gen 12:1–3,[9] are counted as descendants of Abraham (3:6–9), and live within the singular people of God (3:14, 28–29) because of the grace of God (2:21; cf. 5:4).[10] Anyone who has been crucified with Christ (2:20–21; 3:27) may not uphold the very same ethnic barriers that Jesus' death dismantled (3:28). Further,

8. Dunn, 342.
9. The term 'promise' occurs 9x in 3:14–29; cf. 4:23, 28.
10. Hays, 245–48.

any attempt to add a requirement to joining the covenant people is tantamount to nullification of the importance of the death of Christ (2:20–21; cf. 3:1). The death of Jesus is the sole event that makes one right before God and provides entrance into the covenant people of God (Gal 2:15–21; cf. 4:4–7).

On what condition those from differing backgrounds might enter the covenant people is of great consequence in the Letter to the Galatians. Thus, when Paul closes his letter, he addresses the entire church as the Israel of God (6:16). By using the imagery of Israel for Gentile Christians after arguing against circumcision as an entry requirement for Gentiles into the people of God, hearers are reminded of Paul's emphasis that everyone in the covenant community is a recipient of the promise God made to Abram (Gen 12:1–3). Whereas it may sound odd for Paul to refer to Gentile Christians as Israel, his claim is that an uncircumcised Gentile may enter the covenant people of Israel as uncircumcised and should remain uncircumcised. Paul's message is grounded in an understanding that the covenant people of God is one, that the one people begins with God's promise to Abram, and that God's promise to Abram will not fail. God's promise to Abram included blessing upon the nations (Gen 12:3).

Therefore, Gentile Christians should find identity with that blessing, within the people of God, within the Israel of God, only on the basis of the death of Jesus (Gal 2:16, 21; 3:14).

Discussion Questions

1. The phrase Israel of God is used only one time in the Bible. Why do you think Paul emphasizes that Israel is "of God"?

2. Paul read the Hebrew Scriptures as more than just history. Where do you see Paul doing this in the Letter to the Galatians? Can you find examples in other New Testament writings? Can you think of texts in the New Testament that demand our familiarity with Old Testament themes or stories? How might we benefit from Paul's method of reading the Hebrew Scriptures? Why is it important that we know the story of the whole Bible?

3. Trace the theme of promise throughout the Bible. Why do so many books of the Bible return to the theme of God's promise to Abraham? Why does Paul rely on the theme of promise so heavily in Galatians? In what ways is it difficult in our world to believe God keeps promises? Do we have any reminders that God keeps promises? How might understanding God as one who makes promises create identity for God's people today?

4. What is the importance of the death of Jesus in the book of Galatians? In light of this, reflect upon the meaning and implications of the phrase "crucified with Christ" (Gal 2:19) for living the Christian life.

5. In what ways does the book of Galatians and Paul's reference to the church as the Israel of God help us think beyond ourselves as individuals and toward more communal aspects of Christian identity, practice, and obligation?

3

— The Church as Salt and Light —

Bill Bagents

We love Jesus' dynamic description of his church. It's not, "You should be the salt of the earth" or "You have the power to be the light of the world." Rather, the Lord called us to be what he has made us.

We think of salt as flavoring, enriching, and taste-enhancing. Colossians 4:6 comes to mind: "Let your speech always be with grace, seasoned with salt, that you may know how you ought to answer each one". Just as Jesus "went about doing good" (Acts 10:38), so do his disciples. Our conduct and our character enhance our communities. Our presence and examples bring out the best in others. Like Barnabas and Dorcas of old, we should impact those around us for good.

Were we to lose our flavor, our Christian impact, we would fall under the condemnation of Matthew 5:13:

we would be good for nothing. Or perhaps, we'd be even worse. We could distract people from the gospel and give them excuse to live outside Christ. Just as Titus 2:10 calls on servants to "adorn the doctrine of God our Savior in all things," we know the importance of consistently walking "in the light as He is in the light" (1 John 1:7).

Though it is not the point of emphasis in Matthew 5:13, we also think of salt's preserving powers. Salt works against decay and corruption. Spiritual salt works against sin and death. Just as ten righteous souls would have spared Sodom and Gomorrah (Gen 18:32), we are blessed to contemplate the favor that God shows to all because of the presence of His people. It's the principle clearly taught in Genesis 12:1–3.

Fairness demands that we remember that salt also burns at times. Think of getting sweat in your eyes or into a cut as you do outside work on a hot summer's day. In this sin-damaged world, some will regard any spiritual salt as an irritant. They will object to how the presence of salt makes them feel. While it's never our aim to be irritating, sometimes it's a compliment to be considered a bother. It can speak of our distinctiveness in Christ and our faithfulness to Him (1 Pet 4:4; John 3:19–21).

The devil loves debilitating extremes. He will assert that you can't be salt without being salty, overly stout, disagreeable, and painful to others. He will invite some to embrace this model and to ignore John 13:34–35, Ephesians 4:31–32, and Colossians 3:12–17. He will claim that truth trumps grace, love, and kindness. To others, he will invite to purposefully avoid the redeeming qualities of salt, lest they be perceived as negative or judgmental. With them, he will claim that grace, love, and kindness trump truth. How blessed we are to recognize and reject his lies!

We love Jesus' description of us as "the light of the world" (Matt 5:14). This sin-damaged world is plagued by darkness. We see countless examples of what Jesus described as "blind leaders of the blind" (Matt 15:14). Life continually affirms the truth of Jeremiah 10:23 and Proverbs 16:25. Without guidance from above, things don't go well for us.

There's a huge compliment in Matthew 5:14 when Jesus says, "You are the light of the world." Think of John 1:4–5, "In Him was life, and the life was the light of men. And the light shines in the darkness, and the darkness did not comprehend it." Think of John 8:12, "I am the light of the world. He who follows me shall not walk in darkness, but have the light of life." As long as Jesus was in this world in the flesh, he was the light of the world (John 9:5). Now, he describes his followers—his church—with the very same language! "You are the light of the world."

Of course, this is a wonderful testimony of the humility of Jesus. It's also a tremendous statement of his expectation for the church. We are to shine like a city set on a hill. We are to give light to all who are in the house. We are to let our lights so shine that men will see our good works and glorify our Father in heaven.

The second fact about our role as light in this world from Mathew 5:13 is, "A city that is set on a hill cannot be hidden." Christianity was born in a challenging region during a challenging time. The church faced daunting persecution (Acts 8:14; Heb 10:32–34; Rev 2:9–10). Still, Jesus describes his church as "a city set on a hill." The church is, as it were, a lighthouse. It lives, honors, and offers the light of truth and righteousness. It calls people toward the gospel and toward heaven. To use the language of Philippians 2:15, we are "children of God without fault in the midst of a crooked and perverse generation, among whom you shine as lights in the world." That was true in the days of Jesus and Paul. God means for it to be just as true today.

Jesus moves from describing the Christian light as a city on a hill to speaking of it as a lampstand within a home. Its purpose is "to give light to all who are in the house" (Matt 5:14). We give light as we teach and live God's truth. We give light as we love and forgive one another. We give light as we "convince, rebuke, [and] exhort, with all longsuffering and teaching" (2 Tim 4:2). We give light as we "warn the unruly, comfort the fainthearted, uphold the weak, [and] be patient with all" (1 Thess 5:14). We certainly give light as we speak "the truth in love" and "grow up in all things into Him who is the head—Christ." (Eph 4:15).

Matthew 5:16 is both intentional and encouraging. We embrace God's command to let our lights shine. Our good works are purposeful, designed to help others see and honor God. Of course we reject excess and self-centeredness as condemned in Matthew 6:1, 5, and 16. While rejecting pride and self-promotion, we acknowledge the tremendous teaching and motivational power of good works. Even secular people are inclined to believe what they see. It's tremendously challenging to ignore a consistently good and giving life.

The encouraging part of Matthew 5:16 is so easy to grasp. As the church is what the church should be, salt and light in this world, people will see our service in the name of Christ and will give glory to God. We know that a word of caution is needed. Not all will see, and not all who see will choose to glorify God. Some are very skilled at rejecting the Father. But all will have the opportunity to see and give honor. And some will give God the level of honor that includes believing his word and obeying his gospel.

We stand amazed that God gives us the honor of living for him. What a gift to be able to help others recognize and appreciate the Creator, the Ruler of the universe, the Sustainer of all that is good, right, and holy.

We think of light as it enables and enhances vision. We see more clearly in the light. Psalm 119:105 celebrates the truth that, "Your word is a lamp to my feet and a light to my path." Given human frailty, stumbling is a fact of life, but stumbling is lessened by adequate light. Stumbling is also lessened by staying on the path. And stumbling need not be fatal because our God is always there to lift us up.

Admittedly, light can sometimes challenge us. A car can look so clean in the garage, but sunlight shows all the spots and streaks. Our lives can look quite good when compared to the culture around us, but when we examine ourselves in the true Light, what we learn can really scare us. What a joy to remember John 3:16–17, Romans 8, and Ephesians 2:1–10. God's light is ultimate truth and purity. God's light is also stunningly loving. He seeks our best and our salvation. He knows better than we do the dangers and costs of sin (Eph 6:12; Isa 59:1–2). He wants us to learn the joys of living as his church, his children (1 John 3:1–2).

Living as salt and light opens tremendous doors of spiritual opportunity. It's a blessed life here, but the ultimate blessings are unspeakably greater. And those blessings are eternal. Forever. Everlasting. Infinite. Unfathomable.

Discussion Questions

1. What aspect of salt impresses you the most as you think about the church and each individual Christian as "the salt of the earth"?

2. What can we do together and individually to enhance our effectiveness as "the light of the world"?

3. Why would any church or Christian be tempted to hide his/her light?

4. How would a person go about hiding his/her light? What would this look like in practice?

4

From All Eternity

Ted Burleson

What do people generally think of when they hear the word "church"? They may think of several things depending on their backgrounds and comprehension. They may think of a church building, even though the Lord's house actually consists of the people of the church, not the church building (Eph 2:19–22). The building itself is not sacred. Perhaps some people may correctly think of the church in the universal sense and imagine Christians gathering in the name of Christ all over the world. They may mistakenly think of denominational leaders, the pope, or another human leader. Some people's only image of the church may be the pageantry of traditional religious ceremonies and special services. When others hear the word "church," they might accurately think of the church in the local sense and think of local, autonomous congregations in a particular location. Sometimes, because church members are so familiar with congregations on this local level, they might allow petty differences to lead them to make decisions that affect eternity.

This chapter deals with the church from a different view than either the universal or local senses; this lesson considers the church in the eternal sense. The fact is the church has been in God's purpose for all eternity. It is sad to hear some say that because the Jews rejected Jesus, the church was simply a temporary substitute for Christ's kingdom. Perhaps even a majority of Christians has that eschatological (end times) outlook. Nothing could be further from the truth; the church is part of God's eternal purpose. If God has had the church in mind for eternity, it is worth taking the time and effort to consider the church in the eternal sense.

Before we can consider the church, we must consider the actions of its founder and savior, Jesus Christ. Jesus pre-existed in eternity as the Word prior to creation (cf. 1 John 1:1–2, NKJV). Many think of Jesus as only coming into existence in a manger in Bethlehem. However, he exists for all eternity.

When Jesus came to earth, one of his purposes was to make preparations to build his church (cf. Matt 16:18). Christ loved the church so much that he gave himself up for her to fulfill the purposes of God (Eph 5:25; cf. Rom 14:9). God's eternal desire is for a new people, set apart for communion with Him. The church shares in the Great Commission that Jesus gave the apostles shortly before ascending into heaven (cf. Matt 28:18-20).

As members of his body, the church, we are part of God's eternal plan to save the lost. God's ultimate purpose in our salvation is that the church might glorify God's grace for all eternity (Eph 2:7–9; cf. 1:6, 12, 14). Because the church was created for reaching the lost, its primary responsibility is sharing the gospel in an intentional way. The church exists for evangelism, bringing the good news of eternal salvation to all.

One of the clearest teachings about the eternal nature of the church comes from Ephesians 3:8–13, which focuses on God's purpose for the church: preaching the gospel. Paul begins this section of Scripture by explaining how he became a minister according to God's gift of grace (Eph 3:7). Like Paul (although in a different sense), all Christians are also ministers according to God's gift of grace. We each have a responsibility to share the good news of Christ with those with whom we come in contact. If God has had the church in mind for all eternity, it is obvious that it is important to Him. If it was important enough to God for his Son to die for the church, we should encourage others to become part of the church, the body of Christ.

Even though Paul considered himself the least likely to receive it, he received God's grace. Modern Christians may feel inadequate or unqualified to share the gospel. But if Paul, with all his personal baggage from the past, could share the gospel, what could possibly stop Christians from sharing the good news? Paul preached the unsearchable (unfathomable) riches of Christ that was made available to the Gentiles (Eph 3:8). The riches about which Paul writes are so different from worldly riches. Rather, the riches of which Paul writes are those that are eternal in the heavens. Laying up treasure in heaven must include helping others to lay up heavenly treasures as well.

Most people like a good mystery novel or movie. God's mystery is not a mystery in the sense that we have to be very clever to discover clues to get the correct answer. God's mystery was hidden for centuries before it was revealed in Christ. From the beginning of the ages, the mystery was hidden in God (Eph 3:9). Here's the mystery: God's ultimate purpose in our salvation is that the church might eternally glorify God's grace and reach out to bring the lost to Him (cf. Eph 1:6, 12, 14; 2:7–9).

Not only does the church reach out to a lost and dying world, the church reveals God's plan to the spiritual powers including angels and heavenly beings. This fact was in accordance with the eternal purpose God has carried out in Christ Jesus our Lord. Rather than seeing the church as a local group made up of people we know, perhaps it would enhance our view of the church to realize that the church is responsible for educating the angels and other heavenly beings. We know from Scripture that the angels rejoice in heaven when one lost sinner repents (cf. Luke 15:10). Paul also suggests that the angels watch the activities of the local assembly (cf. 1 Cor 11:10).

The angels learn the manifold wisdom of God from the church (Eph 3:10). Of course, the angels know about the power of God as seen in his creation. However, the wisdom of God as seen in his new creation (the church) is something new to them. As the angels watch the outworking of God's salvation, they praise his wisdom. As members of the body of Christ, we are to be faithful stewards of God's great truth. We have God's mystery in our hands.

God's eternal purpose is realized in Christ (Eph 3:11–12). Therefore, in Christ, we can approach God with boldness and have confident access to God through our faith in Him. God's eternal purpose focuses on Christ and his church. This fact should stress the importance of the church as part of God's eternal purpose. Far from being an afterthought, the church is vital for accomplishing God's plan for evangelizing the world. Never think that world evangelism is a thing of the past. As Christians, we must live according to God's eternal vision and purpose for church, and that especially includes evangelism. God is to be glorified in the church (Eph 3:21). We do this best by faithfully following his commands and obeying and practicing the teachings of Jesus.

It is easy to get distracted and think of the church as only a human institution with flaws and defects and become discouraged. Perhaps that is why Paul pleaded with the Ephesians not to lose heart about his suffering on their behalf (Eph 3:13). They should have felt honored and encouraged that Paul was suffering for their sakes. Like our ancient brethren, we must not become disheartened by the struggles of individual, local congregations. We must keep our sight on the eternal nature of the church in God's plan and purpose.

When we think about the church, we should focus on God's eternal purpose and not on our own plans for the church. If we focus on God's eternal purpose for the church, hopefully we will obey his will. Centering our efforts only on our own plans is a sure path to disappointing and disobeying God. Be challenged to think of the church as the fulfillment of God's purpose from all eternity.

Discussion Questions

1. What happens if Christians lose their perspective of the church as being part of God's eternal plan for redeeming humankind and become focused solely upon local troubles and congregational issues?

2. Has the church lost focus of God's plan for the church to preach the gospel to the lost? What can be done to encourage us to get back to this purpose?

3. The mystery hidden in God for the ages was revealed in Christ. Has it again become a mystery to many? What can we as Christians do to reveal the mystery to the lost?

4. How do we find the proper balance between focusing on God's plans for the church and what we know must be done in the local congregation?

5

—A Community of Believers—

Philip Goad

Empty seats. On any given Sunday, most worship assemblies will have some of them—perhaps way too many. Narrow your focus for just a moment to a specific empty seat in your church building. Think about a seat that was once occupied by a faithful brother or sister: a seat that is now vacant not due to death or because someone moved away. That once faithful Christian is simply gone. Disappearances like these often cause us to wrestle with important questions. What went wrong? Did the Christian fail the church family, or did the church family fail the Christian? Could this have been prevented? Is there a way to bring the missing family member back?

What God Wants

In Hebrews 3:12–14, we are reminded that disappearing acts by Christians are not what God wants. He wants every Christian holding fast rather than falling away. Verse 12 reminds us of the value God places on each person when it says, "Take care, brethren, that there not be **in any one of you** an evil, unbelieving heart that falls away" (NASB). Thankfully though, the text also describes God's preventative measure, his divine plan for achieving success. Verse 13 says, "but encourage one another day after day as long as it is still called today." God's planned result is a community of believing hearts who have a commitment to "hold fast the beginning of our assurance firm until the end" (vs. 14). What a blessing it is that God's plan for securing the saved is effective church community!

As such, the big idea for our study is this: every member of a church family has an important role in nurturing the kind of strong Christian community where we are actively helping each other go to heaven.

In spite of God's great plan, many congregations face challenges in achieving success. Attendance boards indicate that Christians are assembling less than they used to. How do members of a community actively encourage each other when the community is spending less time together? How can members be convinced of the value of spending time in community? As shepherds, preachers, and other Christians struggle with questions like these, solutions that work often seem elusive. Could it be, though, that one solution may be much less complicated that we realize?

Meeting People Where They Are

Understanding where people are as they arrive can be valuable in successfully helping them become invested and active in Christian community. This understanding may also help us more successfully create the kind of community that God calls us to be.

- Some think they want God but not the church. The abuses of organized religion have caused some people to be wary.
- Some think it is too risky to admit weakness. As people arrive in community, do they see our congregations as being more like country clubs or more like hospitals?
- Some first arrive as consumers rather than looking for ways to add to and invest in the community. Is it immediately evident that we offer something of value?
- Some are just barely hanging on. People often arrive locked in a daily struggle against being pulled back into the world.
- Some are desperately trying to fit in. Do we make it easy or difficult for new people to find a place in the community to both fit in and be active? Have we honestly assessed the question from a new person's point of view?

Doing Church Community Well

Acts 2:42-47 paints a beautiful picture of vibrant Christian community. The church is new and growing. Excitement is in the air. Worship and prayer are constants. Needs are being met. Apostles are on the scene. Doctrine is being embraced. And the Christians are together...seemingly all the time.

While we love this scene, we also understand that the twenty-first century presents the church of today with challenges in replicating what we read about in Acts 2. While the church is new for the new Christian, the church is no longer new. That "sense of awe" (v. 43) is sometimes lacking. We have the entire Bible rather than apostles, yet doctrine is not always valued. We often do well in meeting needs and in loving each other, but we are challenged in finding ways to get busy, geographically-scattered people to spend an appropriate amount of time together in community. We realize that "daily" is probably out of the question in a practical sense.

In his first book on church growth, *Your Church Can Grow: Seven Vital Signs of a Healthy Church*, C. Peter Wagner presents the idea of experiencing church community at three levels. The first is **celebration**, which refers to what is hopefully a vibrant worship assembly. No matter the size of the assembly, a Christian must worship. The second level is **congregation**, which represents the 30–80 members we know by name, and with whom we regularly spend time in fellowship. Wagner refers to the third level as **cell**, and it may provide the greatest area of opportunity in allowing us to do church community more effectively.[1]

Wagner describes the cell level as the group of 10–12 people who actively help a Christian live out his faith. In other words, this is the group where deeper more interpersonal relationships are formed.[2] Most congregations have groups that fit Wagner's definition of a cell. Some are formally organized while others are not. For example, Bible classes often function as cell groups. The group that eats breakfast together once a week may function as a cell group. The group of people involved in a ministry together, such as benevolence, may function as a cell group. These groups are important because research seems to reflect that church members who are not active in a cell-sized group are most at risk of disappearing from church community.

Consider some of the reasons that these smaller groups are so vital to realizing effective Christian community. First, it is difficult for a Christian to simply disappear, since members of the group will immediately notice his/her absence. Further, it is far less easy

1. C. Peter Wagner, *Your Church Can Grow: Seven Vital Signs of a Healthy Church,* (Ventura, Calif.: Regal Books, 1976), 111–23.
2. Wagner, *Your Church Can Grow*, 123–25.

to be pulled back into the world when there are 10–12 people who are committed to preventing that from happening. In that regard, the close relationships formed in one of these groups make it more difficult for a member of the group to make bad decisions without being challenged biblically by someone in the group. Closeness facilitates accountability.

In his 2012 book, *Why They Left: Listening to Those Who Have Left Churches of Christ*, Flavil R. Yeakley, Jr. references Wagner's work and then provides survey data to illustrate the vital role that close, personal friendships play in effective church community. In his discussion of assimilating new members, Yeakley states, "The most important differences between new members who are assimilated into the congregation and those who drop out of the church are how many close personal friendships they form in the congregation, how many specific church work assignments they are given, and how quickly they are involved in some area of ministry."[3]

In our efforts to effectively live out Hebrews 3:12–14 as a community of believers, it is in our best interest to do everything possible to ensure that every Christian finds a place in some type of a smaller group. But groups must never be perceived as closed circles to

3. Flavil R. Yeakley, Jr., *Why They Left: Listening to Those Who Have Left Churches of Christ,* (Nashville: Gospel Advocate, 2012), 93-4.

those who are trying to find a place. Closed circles become cliques. We must remember that every small group should be open-ended and that most people will not enter the group without an invitation.

God values community. It is, after all, His plan for securing the saved. That is why every member of a church family has an important role in nurturing the kind of strong Christian community where we are actively helping each other go to heaven.

The question becomes, how are we finding our place and helping other people find theirs?

Discussion Questions

1. How would you rate your congregation in the area of "doing" community? Think in terms of "Outstanding," "Average," "Marginal," or "We need an intervention!" Upon what do you base your rating?

2. As a congregation, where are the best opportunities for improvement?

3. How would you encourage a Christian to be active in church community who asserts that he or she wants a relationship with God but not with the church?

4. How many active, cell-size groups can you identify in your congregation? Are they functioning effectively? Why or why not?

6

A Royal Priesthood

C. Wayne Kilpatrick

"But ye *are* a chosen generation, a royal priesthood, a holy nation, a peculiar people; that ye should show forth the praises of him who hath called you out of darkness into his marvelous light" (1 Pet 2:9, KJV).

Just as God distinguished the nation Israel from all other nations, he distinguishes true Christians from the unbelievers. In this passage, Peter describes Christians as a chosen generation, a royal priesthood, a holy nation, a peculiar people, borrowing language from Exodus 19:5–6 where God used similar terms in his description of Israel: "Now, therefore, if ye will obey my voice indeed, and keep my covenant, then ye shall be a peculiar treasure unto me above all people: for all the earth is mine. And ye shall be unto me a kingdom of priests and a holy nation.

These are the words which thou shalt speak unto the children of Israel." Peter was distinguishing the Christian from the disobedient, whether Jew or Gentile. He revealed that Christians, the Israel of God (Gal 6:16), enjoy some of the same privileges as physical Israel did under the Old Covenant.

When Peter wrote that Christians are a "royal priesthood," his parallel is to God's statement to Moses concerning Israel after He had brought them out of Egypt. It seems that God may have originally intended that the entire nation would serve Him as "a kingdom of priests and a holy nation" (Exod 19:1–6). The Levitical priesthood was only instituted because the sin of the people had not yet been atoned; therefore, the sin of Israel as a nation necessitated the intermediary between Israel and God. This was necessary, lest God's holiness "break out like fire in the house of Joseph, and devour *it*, and *there be* none to quench *it* in Bethel" (Amos 5:6). Therefore, God temporarily placed his plan for a "kingdom of priests" on hold.

In Exodus 19:6, the Hebrew expression *mamleketh koh*^{a}*nim* is translated in the KJV as "kingdom of priests." According to Walter Kaiser, there are four correct ways to translate the Hebrew expression into English: "kingdom of priests," "kings that are priests," "priestly kingdom," and "royal priesthood" as Peter wrote.[1]

The promise that Israel would be made a "kingdom of priests" was given to Moses before the Law was given at Mount Sinai. Under the Law of Moses, only descendants of Aaron—from the tribe of Levi—could serve as priests (Exod 28:1), while the perpetual kingship granted to David (2 Sam 7) by necessity elevated to the monarchy only those from Judah's tribe. Therefore, an Israelite could not be both a king and a priest. But before the giving of the Law we have an instance of someone who was both king and priest: "And Melchizedek, king of Salem, brought forth bread and wine; and he was the priest of the most high God" (Gen 14:18). After the establishment of the Law and, with it, the Levitical priesthood, there are some examples of Israelite kings doing the work of priests, such as Saul's offering a sacrifice at Gilgal (1 Sam 13:8–14) or Uzziah's offering incense in the temple (2 Chron 26:16–21). In both instances God shows his displeasure with the kingly usurping of the priestly role.

Just as the nation of Israel was described as a kingdom of priests, so also following the dreaded deed at Calvary, the church has now received this description, having received sanctification through the blood of Jesus. But whereas in reality only descendants of Aaron

1. Walter C. Kaiser, Jr., "Exodus," in *The Expositor's Bible Commentary* (vol. 2; Grand Rapids: Zondervan, 1990), 417.

could serve as priests, all Christians enjoy priestly privileges. Under the Law the high priest alone had access to God, but Christians generally are granted this same access. Even the high priest could enter the Holy of Holies no more than once in a year on penalty of death (Heb 9:7), but Christians may approach boldly at all times through the blood of Christ, without any danger of dying. "Let us, therefore, come boldly unto the throne of grace, that we may obtain mercy, and find grace to help in time of need" (Heb 4:16). The throne of grace is likely the mercy seat on the Ark of the Covenant, located within the Holy of Holies, to which we have constant access through the blood of our High Priest. The writer of Hebrews says:

> Having, therefore, brethren, boldness to enter into the holiest by the blood of Jesus, by a new and living way, which he hath consecrated for us through the veil, that is to say, his flesh; and having a high priest over the house of God; let us draw near with a true heart, in full assurance of faith, having our hearts sprinkled from an evil conscience, and our bodies washed with pure water" (10:19–22).

Access into the holiest (the Holy of Holies) is allowed to all Christians under the gospel, at any time. The tearing of the temple veil at the death of Christ (Matt 27:50–51) symbolized the abolition of the wall separating God from his people.

Now we that are in the "body of Christ" (1 Cor 12:27), are a "royal priesthood," and have been chosen by God himself, we are God's spiritual Israel and a royal priesthood (1 Pet 2:9). Christ, our High Priest, made one sacrifice for sin for all time (Heb 10:12), so that no other sacrifice is needed (Heb 10:26). The priests under the Law of Moses were chosen to serve God with their lives by offering up sacrifices, and we are chosen for the same purpose.

Old Testament sacrifices included a variety of types of offerings, whether burnt offerings (Lev 1), grain offerings (Lev 2), peace offerings (Lev 3), sin offerings (Lev 4), etc. The New Testament spiritual priesthood likewise has a variety of offerings to make. First, there is the sacrifice of praise: "By him, therefore, let us offer the sacrifice of praise to God continually, that is, the fruit of our lips, giving thanks to his name" (Heb 13:15). Even in the Old Testament, Hosea admonishes Israel: "Take with you words, and turn to the Lord: say unto him, Take away all iniquity, and receive us graciously; so will we render the calves of our lips" (Hos 14:2). The praise offered by our mouths Hosea describes as similar to calves offered in sacrifice. Only they of the "royal priesthood" can make this kind of true sacrifice to God. By anyone else the act would be as though Saul himself had offered the sacrifice. Under the New Covenant, we can make the sacrifice of praise at any time.

Another sacrifice Christians make is our obedience, which even in the Old Testament is valued far above animal sacrifices. "And Samuel said, Hath the Lord as great delight in burnt-offerings and sacrifices as in obeying the voice of the Lord? Behold, to obey is better than sacrifice, and to hearken than the fat of rams" (1 Sam 15:22). When we render obedience to God with our lives and conversation, we offer our bodies to be a living sacrifice, holy and acceptable to God, as our reasonable service (Rom 12:1). How do we offer our bodies? We dedicate our lives to the service of God. We become instruments of righteousness unto holiness, by sacrificing ourselves to God. Under the Old Law, only priests could offer sacrifices; but here, we offer our own sacrifices—as the "royal priesthood" of the New Covenant.

Another sacrifice which is offered by the New Covenant priesthood is charity, an expression of Christian love in gifts to others. Jesus says, "And whosoever shall give to drink unto one of these little ones a cup of cold water only in the name of a disciple, verily I say unto you, he shall in no wise lose his reward" (Matt 10:42). Or, again, in Hebrews: "But to do good [deeds] and to communicate, forget not; for with such sacrifices God is well pleased" (Heb 13:16). Our kind, Christian actions are acceptable sacrifices to God.

By these actions, one can see why Peter referred to Christians as a "royal priesthood." We function much like the priest of old in that we offer many kinds of sacrifices to God. The difference is that we can access God through our high priest Jesus Christ at any time—not just once a year in the temple. No matter how insignificant our service may seem, it will be accepted if it is done through faith and obedience and in the name of Jesus Christ. As Paul says, "And whatsoever ye do in word or deed, *do* all in the name of the Lord Jesus, giving thanks to God and the Father by him" (Col 3:17). Christians are truly a "royal priesthood."

Discussion Questions

1. Why did God describe Israel as a kingdom of priests? What would that description have meant to an Israelite?

2. Does Peter's description of the church as a royal priesthood draw a connection between Christians and Israel? What might be the significance of such a connection?

3. In what ways do Christians offer sacrifices to God?

4. How does Peter's phrase "royal priesthood" help you to understand the purpose of the Christian life?

7

A Holy Nation

Brad McKinnon

As I'm writing this essay, the President of the United States has just concluded his State of the Union Address. There are few spectacles that highlight the complexities of the modern nation-state more than this annual speech to Congress. The House and the Senate, the Supreme Court, the Executive Branch—all represented in this rather strange interplay of often disparate voices within the nation. So, what is a nation?

We may picture the modern nation-state with its complex government bureaucracy, powerful military, and market economy. Or, we may simply think of a people bound together by a common history, ethnicity, language, culture, religion, or even an idea.

It wasn't complex bureaucracies that brought Israel together in the hot and arid Sinai Peninsula at the base of a rugged mountain in Exodus 19. Rather, it was a common history and culture centered around an idea: that the Lord was Israel's God and that he had acted on their behalf as a people. Along with these blessings came certain expectations. Listen to how both these blessings and responsibilities are described: "You have seen what I did to the Egyptians, and how I bore you on eagles' wings and brought you to myself. Now therefore, if you obey my voice and keep my covenant, you shall be my treasured possession out of all the peoples. Indeed, the whole earth is mine, but you shall be for me a priestly kingdom and a holy nation" (Exod 19:4–6, NRSV).

Several built-in points seem apparent in these brief verses. First, the concept of **covenant** stands out. A covenant can be defined as a formal agreement between two or more parties in which each promise to act in certain ways. But *which* covenant? Was it the covenant God had made with Abraham in the past or a covenant that he was about to make with the people moving forward? It's probably safe to assume here that this is a case of both/and, rather than either/or. In Exodus 2:24–25, we are told that the basis for Israel's salvation from Egyptian slavery was that God remembered the covenant that he had made with Abraham. That covenant is described in Genesis 12.

In short, God would make of Abraham a great nation, bless those who blessed him, and through

Abraham bless all nations. Therefore, Israel would keep the covenant by remembering that as the special children of Abraham, they had certain responsibilities to become a blessing. The subsequent laws that formed the basis for these responsibilities are naturally described as "the book of the covenant" (Exod 24:7). Thus, as God promised to bless Abraham, he was continuing to do so through the nation of Israel and expected them to respond appropriately.

Second, the text describes what should be their motivation for such a response: they were to remember what God had done for them (Exod 19:4). The Exodus was the great salvation story for Israel. Ingrained in their minds from generation to generation through the annual Passover feast, when the people of Israel thought of salvation, they instinctively thought of communal redemption.

Likewise, as the church, we shouldn't forget that while we have an individual responsibility to God, this cannot be detached from our responsibility to each other in community. Rather, seeing after each other follows the example of Christ and connects us to God more deeply. Notice how Paul connects our vertical relationship with Christ with the horizontal relationship we as Christians have with each other: "Let each of you look not to your own interests, but to the interests of others. Let the same mind be in you that was in Christ Jesus" (Phil 2:4–5). The "eagles' wings" imagery in

Exodus 19 would be used later in Israel's history in a context of captivity and redemption (Isa 40:31).

The notion is clear: God had acted and would continue to act to help Israel rise above its difficulties, even when those difficulties were, at times, of their own making. Importantly, these promises were conditional based on certain expectations: "if" you obey my voice and keep my covenant (Exod 19:5). This underscores the humility of God. While he could force people to bend to his will by brute force (as in the Exodus), Israel had the freedom to choose to serve him or not.

This service had a missional component as well, it seems. It wasn't just Israel that belonged to God, but rather "the whole earth" or "all the peoples." The text describes Israel's national function as that of a priest ("priestly kingdom"). Israel was to be a means through which other nations could relate to God. These values were to infuse all aspects of national life ("holy nation"). Their religion, culture, economy, and even politics were expected to be holy. Holiness indicates that something or someone had been dedicated for sacred use.

Soon after the Exodus experience, the concept of holiness took on strong moral connotations too. Leviticus 20:7 exhorts the people to "be holy; for I am the Lord your God." What did that necessitate? Observe the statutes: don't kill; don't steal; don't curse father and mother; don't commit adultery (Lev 20:9ff.). These expectations would see Israel through victory and defeat; conquest and captivity; generation after generation.

Now fast forward to the time of the early church. First, Peter argues that Abraham's covenant fulfilled in Israel was continuing in the church: "... you are a chosen race, a royal priesthood, a holy nation, God's own people, in order that you may proclaim the mighty acts of him who called you out of darkness into his marvelous light" (1 Pet 2:9). The first half of the verse is a quotation of Exodus 19:6. Just as Israel had come to Sinai after fleeing Egypt and had received divine instructions, Peter sees his Gentile readers ("you were ransomed from the futile ways inherited from your ancestors"; 1 Pet 1:18) as ready to take their place in God's story that had been established "before the foundation of the world" (1 Pet 1:20).

A modern evangelical emphasis on individual salvation sometimes causes us to read into the biblical text a bold distinction between personal and communal holiness that was not obvious in a first century context. So what does Peter have in mind when he refers to his readers as a "holy nation"? What does that look like on the ground? Certainly, this included personal holiness. Peter exhorts his readers to be holy in all their conduct by rejecting their former desires (1 Pet 1:13–15). But he also expects social holiness. They were to conduct themselves honorably within the society that they lived (1 Pet 2:11–25). Finally, he sees the importance of communal holiness. They were to rejoice in righteous suffering together as part of the household of God (1 Pet 4:12–19).

As the household or family of God, Peter sees the church as part of the continuing story of what God is doing in this world. The church highlights the sovereignty of God. Just like he chose Israel for his purposes, he has chosen the church as his people. As God's people, we are called to live out God's reign: "Your will be done, on earth as it is in heaven" (Matt 6:10).

It isn't unusual around the Fourth of July holiday to see the first half of Psalm 33:12 ("Blessed is the nation whose God is the Lord") posted on church signs or quoted from pulpits. The implication is that if the United States will once again make the Lord its God, then it will be happy or blessed. Unfortunately, this sort of interpretive approach doesn't take into account the second half of the verse which includes the parallel statement: "the people whom he has chosen as his heritage." This is the equivalent of "my treasured possession out of all peoples" in Exodus 19. That nation was ancient Israel and continues in the church as the reconstituted people of God today—a nation without borders, you might say. This myth of American sanctity sees national prosperity as an indication of righteousness, thus understanding economic, political, or military power as a sign of divine favor. On the contrary, seeing ourselves as "exiles" as 1 Peter suggests (2:11) allows us, no matter the political landscape in which we find ourselves, to proclaim the power of God, who called us from darkness to light (2:9).

Discussion Questions

1. How does the concept of a "holy nation" help us see ourselves as part of the larger story that God has been telling for millennia?

2. What dangers are there in seeing covenant passages through the lens of American political, military, and economic power?

3. In what ways can the Reformation sentiment of universal priesthood ("the priesthood of all believers") inform our ideas of what it means to be the people of God today?

4. How well do you feel today's church is fulfilling its purpose to be a "holy" nation?

8

—The Church and Worship—

Jeremy Barrier and Lori Eastep

Like a cut gem, the church has many facets. But arguably the most fundamental facet, and the most recognizable to the outside world, is that of worship. In this chapter, we'll explore what worship is, what it does, and how it impacts our spiritual lives.

Worship Is an Act of Humility

The formality, intellectual humor, and accents on BBC television are fascinating. One thing that always stands out is the deference with which the lords and ladies of old Britain are treated. They never enter a room without a flurry of bows and curtsies, head nods, and tipped hats.

There's something majestic about it, something regal, and its stands in sharp contrast to modern society.

We've built an egocentric generation insistent on its own rights and cultivated a culture in which personal happiness and individual desires trump the happiness and desires of all others. As the saying goes, "We bow to no one." And though there's no doubting the blessing that comes with that ultimate freedom, it is perhaps an unintended consequence that we struggle with the idea of worship as an act of humility.

There's a dizzying amount of "falling down" that occurs in Scripture. Time and again, when introduced to God made flesh, individuals fall down and worship him (Matt 2:11; 9:18; 15:25; 28:9). They recognize that something remarkable is taking place before their eyes, and that they've entered into the presence of someone greater than themselves. In our worship, too, we are recognizing the presence of someone greater than ourselves, figuratively kneeling before the Father. J. Oswald Sanders said, "In the act of worship, God communicates His presence to His people."[1] And that presence is worthy of our awe and adoration.

The Greek word *proskuneo*, used 60 times in the New Testament, is most often translated "to worship" or "to bow down." The word is a compound of two parts together meaning, "kissing the hand toward"; it's derived from the idea of a dog licking his master's

1. As cited in Ed Stetzer and Thom S. Rainer, *Transformational Church* (Nashville: Broadman and Holman, 2010), 156.

hand. It's not an image that would be considered attractive to the average twenty-first century American, but what an excellent way to describe the meekness with which we approach the throne of the Almighty—with boldness, yes (Heb 4:16), but also with the submissive attitude that allowed the Christ to pray, "Not as I will, but as you will" (Mark 14:36).

Worship Is a Public Declaration

Acts 4:32–37 is one of the most fascinating texts in Scripture. The passage introduces the reader to Barnabas, who was known for his encouraging leadership and his great benevolence. In this passage, Barnabas sells a piece of land and gives the proceeds from the sale to the church so that they can distribute the funds to feed, clothe, and house the community of Christians gathered in Jerusalem. One of the key moments is found in verses 32–34:

> Now the whole group of those who believed were of one heart and soul, and no one claimed private ownership of any possessions, but everything they owned was held in common. With great power the apostles gave their testimony to the resurrection of the Lord Jesus, and great grace was upon them all. There was not a needy person among them.

On first glance, it's a bit confusing that we jump from the principles of the believers having "one heart and soul" to the apostles preaching sermons, then to believers selling land and giving to the needy. How are these three seemingly separate ideas connected in the mind of the author? After some thought, however, the mental leaps become clear. The believers' worship was something that happened frequently, with purpose, and this was the one time when all three of these events in the text were most clearly displayed. Christians gathered together, and you could *see* how they were connected in their hearts and souls. You could *see* them lifting up God in praise of Jesus, the resurrected one. You could *see* them giving of their funds to help the needy. Meeting regularly as an institution is one of the ways that we, as people of faith, make a public declaration to our communities and the world that we are here to have a single purpose. We are here to lift up our God. We are here to say to our community, "If you are needy, come."

Worship Should Be An Act of Sincerity

Most of you can probably quote Isaiah 29:13, just as Jesus did (Matt 15:8): "These people honor me with their lips, but their hearts are far from me." Nothing frustrated Jesus more than insincere worshippers, and the Scriptures are full of his admonitions to set aside the rote and the ritual for something better, something more complete. But my favorite line of Isaiah's passage comes in verse 16, when he says, "You turn things upside down!" When we go through the motions of worship and fail to engage our hearts, or when we faultily assume that our attendance "checkbox" has earned us points in God's eyes, we've got our worship turned upside down. It's like offering someone a wrapped box with no gift inside.

In Zechariah 7:5–6, God asks the Israelites, "When you fasted and mourned in the fifth and seventh months for the past seventy years, was it really for me that you were fasting? And when you were eating and drinking, were you not just feasting for yourselves?" In layman's terms, *Is your heart in it? Is this for me or for you?* God has always been just as concerned with our motives as He is with our actions. And he asks each of us, *Is your heart in it? Is this for me or for you?*

The bad news is that the Israelites had the wrong answer. "They refused to pay attention," continues Isaiah 7:11. "Stubbornly they turned their backs and stopped up their ears." They were fulfilling their obligations physically, but spiritually, they had disengaged. The good news is that each of us gets to choose. No matter the "worship atmosphere" of your congregation, no matter what the people around you are doing, you get to choose the aroma of your sacrifice of praise to God (Heb 13:15).

And when our actions come from a place of sincerity, good things necessarily follow. Our worship becomes purer, deeper, and more joyful. We read in Acts 2:46 of the early Christians who met together with "glad and sincere hearts," and the very next verse describes the daily (yes, daily!) additions to the body of believers. Why? Sincere worship is contagious. C.S. Lewis once said, "It is frustrating to have discovered a new author and not to be able to tell anyone how good he is"[2]. In the same way, when we begin to truly worship the Almighty, when we have tasted that the Lord is good (Psa 34:8), our desire to share him will naturally grow.

Worship As a Part of Life

Finally, as an extension of the idea that worship is an act of humility, worship is part of who we are. We are constantly living in a state of awareness that there is a God, and we are not him! I vividly remember hearing the preacher Charles Hodge's simple and profound prayer: "Dear God, You are God, and I am not!" This prayer can be developed into an attitude that can be taken with us wherever we go. One of the best passages dealing with worship as a lifestyle has to be the parable of the Good Samaritan in Luke 10:29–37. As the story goes, there was a man who was on his way to Jericho, having left Jerusalem, when he was robbed, beaten and left for dead on the road. Two men passed by him, did not help him and kept going. The third person to pass was the one who helped him: this was the Samaritan.

2. C.S. Lewis, *Reflections on the Psalms* (London: Harcourt Brace, 1958; New York: HarperCollins, 2017), 111. Citation refers to the HarperCollins edition.

The first and second men, a priest and Levite respectively, were employed in the daily service of the Temple. This means that they not only coordinated worship times, but that they tended to the noncorporate facets of Temple life as well—in essence, service for the Temple that was not a direct worship to God. The Samaritan was not employed in such a profession, and by definition of being a "Samaritan," he would not have even attended worship times at the Temple (see John 4:20). In short, the irony here is that those who should have understood how important it is to honor God every day, did not. The one who did not understand the importance of the Temple in Jerusalem, did understand worship and service to God on a daily basis.

Worship is more than a ritual we perform during a particular hour of a particular day. Our corporate services are only the beginning, only a starting point, for the sincere, humble, worshipful manner of our lives. May we not forget that God cares about our attitude every day, and not only on Sunday.

Discussion Questions

1. What is the purpose of worship?

2. How does the New Testament describe proper Christian worship?

3. Does worship have a role in evangelism?

4. What are some specific steps we can take to ensure that our worship is not “upside down” or insincere?

9

—Care of Widows and Orphans—

Michael Jackson

The God of Israel is the protector and provider for orphans and widows. The psalmist writes, “A father of the fatherless and a judge for the widows, is God in his holy habitation” (Psa 68:5, NASB). In the Old Testament, the Law required that remnants of the harvest be left in the fields for orphans and widows to glean (Deut 24:19). Every third year, widows and orphans were invited to partake of the tithe of produce from that year (Deut 14:28–29). Obeying these commandments brought blessing. Ignoring them brought cursing: “Cursed is he who distorts the justice due an alien, orphan, and widow” (Deut 27:19).

Orphans and widows were protected members of community life and valued as important in the eyes of the LORD. “You shall not afflict any widow or orphan. If you afflict him at all, and if he does cry out to me, I will surely hear his cry" (Exod 22:22–24). The protection from the community was to flow from God's own protection and care, "The LORD protects the strangers; He supports the fatherless and the widow, But He thwarts the way of the wicked" (Psa 146:9).

In the Old and New Testaments, orphans and widows are often spoken of together as those in need of special provision from God and his people. James states that "pure and undefiled religion in the sight of our God and Father is this: to visit orphans and widows in their distress" (Jam 1:27). Thus, as would be expected, God's desire for the church is to be the facilitator of his nature—caring for and protecting widows and orphans.

Besides the passage in James 1:27, orphans are only discussed in a metaphorical sense in the New Testament. In Jesus' discussion of the Spirit in John 14, he promises the disciples that he will "not leave them as orphans" (John 14:18). Paul, in 1 Thessalonians 2:17, speaks of "having been orphaned" (my translation) from the Thessalonians for a short while, where he simply means separated by space and company.

Widows, on the other hand, occupy a more prominent place in the New Testament. In the story of the widow's mite in Mark 12:41–44, the widow, who gives two small copper coins of very little value, becomes the hero of Jesus' teaching because she gives "all she had to live on." This illustrates both Jesus' admiration for her sacrificial service to God, as well as the plight of poverty that widows often faced.

Jesus, having already referenced the widow of Zarephath story in Luke 4:25–26, proceeds to revive a widow's son in Luke 7:12. What is surprising in this story is that the son is not being brought to Jesus. Jesus notices the funeral procession at the gate of the city and has compassion for the deceased's mother, the widow. He could not keep from helping her. Jesus did not appreciate the scribes who "devour widows' houses" (Luke 20:47). We see in Jesus what we would expect to see from God in the flesh, carrying out his Father's desire to care for and respect those who are less fortunate.

The church has, and will always, struggle with finding the most effective and appropriate means for caring for the less fortunate. In the New Testament, one particular passage highlights the difficulties the early Christian communities faced as they cared for widows. This passage is of supreme importance for the Lord's church today if we are to see how to proceed in caring for the underprivileged.

The passage comes from the Book of Acts and describes the effort of the earliest disciples to adapt to the needs of widows in the community. In Acts 6:1–7, we see that even as the church was in its infancy, there was already a process for caring for widows. This process, most likely, was a carry-over from the current Jewish practice called *tamhuy*, which was the name of the tray on which food was placed for distribution. However, this could also be referring to a financial distribution that was handed out from the *quppah*, the name of the box that was used to collect funds for distribution to those in need each week. At any rate, some widows within this growing Christian community were feeling neglected during this distribution of food or money.

This problem that arose in the early church was a good one. The text makes it clear that the issue arose because the church "was increasing in number" (Acts 6:1) and that the resolution of the problem resulted in further growth (Acts 6:7). Greek-speaking Jewish-Christian widows were experiencing neglect based upon the language and cultural barriers that they faced interacting with Aramaic-speaking Jewish Christians.

This passage of scripture is significant for a few reasons: (1) Luke chooses to share with us that care for widows (and the less fortunate) was an integral part of the early church. The early church was a community known for its sharing, so much so that Luke could say that "there was not a needy person among them" (Acts 4:34). This highlights how important it was to the disciples when it was discovered that those in need were being neglected. (2) The practice of the early Christians, which appears to derive from their Jewish custom, was to provide daily for short-term needs. Whenever this system became out of balance or was not working equally for all of the widows, it was important enough for the Twelve to call a meeting and seek for a community solution to the matter (Acts 6:2). (3) The church's decision to appoint seven men of outstanding reputation to carry out the work of service to widows demonstrates the importance of good servant leadership in carrying out such a vital work. In the cases of Stephen and Philip, we see two servant leaders who not only cared for widows, but also became integral in the progression of God's Word to the world (Acts 7–8). What practical suggestions might we glean from these observations?

Do We Care Like God Cares?

The first practical suggestion for the local church to ask itself is, "Are we caring for orphans and widows (and the less fortunate among us) in the way that God would want us to?" The entire foundation of our Christian practice comes from better understanding God and his nature. We have demonstrated that Israel and the early church understood the significance of caring for widows and orphans because God demanded it in their communities. How well are we doing in our churches? What actions are demonstrating that we care the way God cares?

Do We Adapt Our Solutions to the Challenges of Service?

Just as the early disciples had to work through their circumstances in order to meet the needs of widows and orphans, so do we. In your congregation, it may not be that one certain group of widows is being neglected; it may be that *all* are being neglected. It may be that your local church has not thought about or reflected on the needs of orphans. Or, it may not be that widows are being neglected, it may simply be that their needs have changed. Is the church gathering together as a community to address these needs? Society has changed in so many ways, so what are we doing to ensure that widows and orphans in our churches have their basic needs provided for? Are our methods working, or do we need to adjust them to ensure we are both meeting needs and growing the church?

Do We Appoint Servant Leaders for the Vital Guidance Needed?

Many times, it's not that we don't care, or even that we don't reflect on the consequence of not serving orphans and widows. Often, it is simply that we have not identified good servant leaders to carry out the work. Servant leaders, like Stephen or Philip, don't lead from the boardroom—they lead with their hands and feet. They are able to recruit fellow workers, rather than manage indentured servants. They are leaders precisely because of their ability to care for orphans and widows because they know that is what God desires for them to do. They aren't afraid to ask the hard questions mentioned above. Perhaps most of all, they aren't afraid of making mistakes and learning from trying. These are the types of servant leaders that churches should seek to delegate the essential task of caring for orphans and widows.

Discussion Questions

1. Why do you think that God gives some responsibility for caring for orphans and widows to His community (first Israel, now the church)?

2. What were Jesus' feelings toward the less fortunate, including orphans and widows? Discuss the ways in which Jesus' views regarding those who were less fortunate translated into action and service.

3. What were the issues that arose in the early church regarding serving widows? How did the church resolve those challenges?

4. Is there only one right way for a local church to care for widows and orphans? If so, what way is it? If not, why not?

10

Such Were Some of You

Rusty Pettus

My high school recently had our twentieth-year reunion. I didn't go, but I did enjoy everyone posting "then" and "now" pictures of themselves on Facebook. It is fun to look back and see our hairstyles and the clothes we wore.

Every generation experiences this change of fashion. You may have worn plaid jackets, hot pants, polyester suits, acid-washed jeans, or some other fad. You may have worn a mullet, high top fade, slicked your hair back with Brylcreem, had a bouffant, a beehive, or used a full can of hairspray while you teased your hair to get it bigger and bigger.

When we see those old pictures, we cringe at how ridiculous we looked. We laugh and think, "How did we ever think that was cool?" But we did, and we were proud of it! When we wore a red leather jacket with one glove, we thought we looked amazing. But now, not so much.

What would you think if one day, some of your friends began to dress the way they did in high school? Maybe they would start it as a joke for one night, but then they would continue dressing that way every day. As part of their daily routine, perhaps they would wear a polyester suit, platform shoes, or a red Members Only jacket. Or one day you notice they are growing a mullet that would make Billy Ray Cyrus proud. You would probably be a little embarrassed for them, and maybe have a talk to ask them what is going on that is making them revert back to the fashion of their youth. We would be a little worried, and maybe even suggest they see a counselor. "Retro" may be in, but shoulder pads and disco are not.

In 1 Corinthians we meet a church that isn't guilty of returning to the fashion of their youth, but to the sins they committed before they came to faith in Jesus. Before we go further, I want you to think about what it would be like for you to go to a foreign country where there is no church or concept of Christianity. You are able to convert 40 people. Some of them worshiped idols, cheated on their wives, were dishonest businessmen, were morally bankrupt. Now they are

Christians, but they don't really know how to worship God. Can you imagine what that church could look like? Maybe Bob only knows how to worship Apollos, so he brings a little of that into the church. Mary worshiped Aphrodite and she wants to bring those customs to the assembly. Johnny only worshiped money, and Suzy was part of a cult religion. This may give us some insight as to what the church of Corinth could have struggled with.

When we read 1 Corinthians, we see a church characterized by abandonment of spouses, conflict among different social classes, adultery—in one case—with a step-mother, jealousy over spiritual gifts, crazed and competitive worship services, and more. In chapters five and six, Paul addresses members who are returning to their former sins, members who are making bad business deals and are suing one another, and even a man who is involved in an incestuous relationship. Paul tells them that surely, they can find wise and honest people in their church who could act as arbiters and avoid making a public scene. Then he calls them to remember their history:

> Do you not know that wrongdoers will not inherit the kingdom of God? Do not be deceived! Fornicators, idolaters, adulterers, male prostitutes, sodomites, thieves, the greedy, drunkards, revilers, robbers—none of these will inherit the kingdom of God. And this is what some of you used to be (1 Cor 6:9–11a).

Paul may be speaking in general or he could be remembering specific members and the sins they were involved in before they knew Jesus. This is no whitewashed version, but a raw version of who they used to be. When we read this, we can't help but see the power of Jesus. These people are no "choirboys"—these are the people your mother warned you not to hang out with. However, that is not who they *are*, but who they *used to be*.

Their transformation should remind us never to count someone out by thinking that they could never become a Christian. We need to remember that there is power in the good news of Jesus; it has the power to save people! Sometimes we trust too much in ourselves. We think, "I could never convert him," "I could never change her," or "I could never talk to or teach him." Often, we make evangelism too much about us. But the power is in Jesus, not me. I am not capable of changing anyone, but God can. I am not their Savior, Jesus is. We have to decide to quit making conversion about *my* knowledge, *my* ability, or *me*. It is about Jesus. The people at Corinth had changed. They used to be sinners, but that was before they met Jesus.

As my classmates and I were posting memories online prior to our class reunion, I received a call from a former classmate. He and I had a class together in high school and became friends. He wasn't the "poster child" for Jesus, to say the least. Our conversations in high school were usually about his antics and the trouble that had ensued. He drank too much and got into a fight; he was with a girl who thought she may be pregnant; he stole something and almost got caught. You get the idea. When he called, my heart skipped a beat, as I didn't know what to expect. I really didn't want to take the phone call. I thought about ignoring it because I didn't want to stroll down Memory Lane and remember the past. He asked me what I was doing these days and I told him I was a youth minister. He got a good laugh and told me that he "could see that." Then he told me something that took me aback: he was a deacon at his church. "Your church? You go to church?" I wanted to ask if I was talking to the right person. He had been washed, sanctified, and justified in the name of the Lord Jesus Christ and in the Spirit of our God.

If I were to be honest, I would never have believed he would give his life to Jesus. I never talked to him about Jesus. He was a sinner. Not *just* a sinner—he was one of the chief sinners (sound familiar?). If our class had given the "Most Likely To Go To Jail" superlative, he would have won it, hands down. But an example like this is what makes the gospel amazing. It contains the power to penetrate the calloused heart. It has the power to wash away every sin. Sometimes we forget how powerful the gospel is.

Paul continues in 1 Cor 6:11 by reminding them of the moment that they put away their old ways of sin, and put on Jesus: "But you were washed, you were sanctified, you were justified in the name of the Lord Jesus Christ and in the Spirit of our God." He wants them to remember their baptism: they were washed; they were justified. Paul constantly takes his readers back to their baptism to remind them of the covenant they made with God and the new life that results from it. In Romans 6:3–7, he says,

> Do you not know that all of us who have been baptized into Christ Jesus were baptized into his death? Therefore we have been buried with him by baptism into death, so that, just as Christ was raised from the dead by the glory of the Father, so we too might walk in newness of life. For if we have been united with him in a death like his, we will certainly be united with him in a resurrection like his. We know that our old self was crucified with him so that the body of sin might be destroyed, and we might no longer be enslaved to sin. For whoever has died is freed from sin.

When we were baptized, we put to death our selfish desires, we renounced our sins, we changed the way we think, and we decided to take on the ways of Jesus. As a result, our sins were washed away, and God declared us justified (innocent) in his eyes. To Paul, baptism is when we embody the life of Jesus and participate in his death, burial, and resurrection. We sacrifice our life and give it to God. We die to our sinful desires and come up out of the water as a new creation who now lives a new life. Paul reminds us that we were washed, we were justified or pronounced innocent, and we were sanctified or set apart from the world. We are to be holy as God is holy, and no longer live and think like the world (1 Pet 1:15-16). We cannot conform to the world but be transformed by renewing our minds every day (Rom 12:2). We cannot revert back to our past but must keep growing closer to Jesus every day.

In Colossians, Paul follows his thoughts on how baptism changes us to say we have put to death fornication, impurity, evil desires, and greed. He also says that we have stripped off our old self, and now we dress in new attire that is being renewed in knowledge according to the image of our Creator. Paul is basically telling us that it is time to take get rid of the shoulder pad blouses, cut off the mullet, and put the platform shoes in the yard sale. Those things may have made us who we used to be, but now we are to put on our whitewashed robes and live for Jesus.

Discussion Questions

1. What are some things that you used to wear but now find embarrassing or at least amusing? What has changed over the last several years to make you decide that those are no longer fashionable?

2. As we mature in our faith, we should begin to see sin as God does instead of from a human perspective.

When we see sin from God's point of view, how does it look different?

3. What is it about our past sins that can draw us back to them and pull us to our old lives?

4. How do we help people understand the significance that Paul gives baptism in Romans 6?

11

Equipping the Saints

Jim Collins

Many years ago, I made the decision to serve my country in the Army National Guard. I was fresh out of high school. The country was in the midst of the Vietnam War. I learned many important things from military service that have provided me with a good foundation for life. The military has a tried and proven method of preparing people for going to war and battling the enemy. These include the necessity of good attitudes and individual preparation, fighting with the vitality of purpose, and winning the war. These goals of the army remind me of Paul and his commitment to train God's soldiers for winning the war in Ephesus.

The Apostle Paul is writing to the church at Ephesus on the "how to" for church unity. He stresses (a) the essential attitudes needed, (b) individual preparation, and (c) the vitality of purpose to be successful and win the war. Just as the Ephesians were in a spiritual war in the first century, we are still experiencing that same war today. As long as the Lord allows the earth to stand, we will always be fighting a war with Satan. Peter warned, "Be sober, be vigilant, because your adversary the devil walks about like a roaring lion, seeking whom he may devour" (1 Pet 5:8, NKJV). How does he go about it? He seeks to destroy Christians individually and the church collectively through pride, selfishness, and division. He uses these negative attitudes to diminish the effectiveness of the body, destroy a Christian's influence, and create division where he can. No one is immune. This is why it is important for every Christian to study, pray, and be equipped for battle.

Honestly, Satan has succeeded in many places among many good spiritual people who let down their guard and are not equipped for the war. So how do we remedy this problem? Let's consider the advice given to the church at Ephesus by the Apostle Paul.

The Essentiality of Attitude (Eph. 4:1-6)

The Apostle Paul describes the necessity of certain attitudes for success in the war with Satan. This is one of the first things military training seeks to establish within each individual. We are a unit; we work together, serve a common cause, help each other go, fight, and win. Paul describes the beginning of this attitude as "I, therefore the prisoner of the Lord, beseech you to **walk worthy of the calling** with which you were called" (Eph 4:1).

The question is, as followers of Christ, how will you and I act or react in our Christian walk on a daily basis? How will we choose to respond to life's daily struggles, stresses, trials, and tribulations? How will we deal with others who may be full of controversy, criticism, ugliness, or just meanness, whether Christians or non-Christians? If I want to respond with a Christ-like disposition, I must take action to incorporate these certain attitudes as an essential part of my Christian life. If you haven't made an effort to put good attitudes in, they won't come out.

So what are these essential attitudes? Paul states that one is humility (a combination of lowliness and gentleness; Eph 4:2). When we incorporate humility into our lives, it allows us to act in direct opposition to worldly or ungodly responses. The worldly response is fueled with pride, arrogance, and high mindedness. Regardless of what you call these responses, the meaning is still the same. In other words, you can paint a tiger white, but he is still a tiger.

Secondly, Paul includes "patience" (Eph 4:2). Perhaps the word "longsuffering" is more applicable. It conveys an attitude of more than patient endurance or putting up with people who have a difficult personality. It's the idea of being long suffering with a hope for a good outcome as a result of your being Christ-like in your actions. Christ-like action is much more likely to bring about good results and cause spiritual growth in you and your brother.

A third essential attitude is that of "bearing with one another in love" (Eph 4:2). Love is a positive action, not a negative reaction. As with any significant relationship, love allows it to be more than expected. Love is going the second and third mile in order to achieve winning the person over and accomplish God's purpose, while we strive to be the Lord's servant. It's walking worthy of the sacrifice made by the Lord Jesus Christ, while trying to be like Christ (Phil 2:5).

One scholar states, "When we read of the story of Pentecost, the picture is one of a group, united in a confession of faith, and then empowered by the 'Spirit' of the risen Christ, now no longer present in His resurrection body, but present nevertheless in a new person form."[1]

A fourth attitude is a "unification" theme and enhanced by the oneness concept. "There is one body, one Spirit, one hope, one Lord, one faith, one baptism, one God and Father of all, and through all, and in you all" (Eph 4:4–6). Can you imagine a military unit going to battle without unity? Going to war without unity is

1. The Expositor's Bible Commentary, vol. 11, Ephesians-Philemon, p. 684-85.

welcoming disaster to the unit. Why would we expect the church—his body—to be successful without unity?

The Individuality of Equipping (Eph 4:11-12)

Paul declares there are differing gifts among the members of the body, the church. These gifts are given individually for the equipping of the Saints and the overall effectiveness of the church. This is a continuous theme throughout the scriptures, always relevant. Just think if everyone in the military was trained to do the exact same job. It would be chaos in the making. I served first in a scout unit, attached to a tank unit. When the scout unit was eliminated, I was required to learn all of the different tasks associated with a tank: loader, driver, gunner, and tank commander.

The Christian life is similar. The Parable of the Talents (Matt 25:14–30) depicts individuals using their talents (money, but symbolically representing our different abilities) in order to be productive for the Master. Paul told the church in Corinth about the body concept: "For as the body is one and has many members, but all the members of that one body, being many, are one body, so also is Christ" (1 Cor 12:12). He also states the need of using the body (members) and their gifts effectively for the benefit of the whole body (1 Cor 12:27). Paul says similarly in Romans, "so we, being many are one body in Christ, and individually members of one another. Having then gifts differing according to the grace that is given to us, let us use them" (Rom 12:5-6). He continues by describing the gifts. What we have learned?

- We are all part of the church—the body of Christ—and we have been equipped with different gifts/talents. We need to identify these gifts and put them to use in his body, the church. When we start using our talents for God, Christ, and his church, God will help us develop other gifts or talents (Matt 25:20-24). To fail to use them for God's glory is to be like the one-talent man who was afraid and hid his master's gift in the ground (Matt 25:24-30).
- And as Paul stated in (Eph 4:12), the body (the church) is prepared "for the equipping of the saints for the work of the ministry, for the edifying (building up) of the body of Christ."

The Vitality of Purpose

The Apostle so beautifully describes the purpose of the gifts, but also goes on to describe, in detail, the vital purpose of those who have the gift of working within the church. These are the end results of a church working effectively:

- Becoming unified in faith and knowledge of the Son of God.
- Becoming a more perfect person and obtaining a higher level of spiritual maturity. We will no

longer be like children who are tossed to and fro by every doctrine that comes along.

- Learning to speak the truth in love and grow upward toward Christ.
- Individual members not only grow, but the church also grows as a spiritual body: "joined and knit together by what every joint supplies, according to the effective working by which every part does its share, causes growth of the body for the edifying of itself in love" (Eph 4:16).

Discussion Questions

1. How does the Apostle Paul describe the way we should act as Christians?

2. Give three words to describe the essential attitudes needed for growth.

3. How would you describe the end result of a well-equipped church?

4. What is the ultimate goal or purpose of a unified church?

12

— The Mission of the Church —

Travis Harmon

In the famous passage in Matthew 16:18, Jesus states that he will establish his church, and in Acts 2 we see the fulfillment of that promise. Peter preaches that Jesus was the Savior, and that he had been crucified and resurrected. Many people believe and respond. Acts 2:40 states that about 3,000 souls were added to their number that day. The church is established in a big way, but now what? What are those people to do now? The church has never existed before. So what is this church to do?

We probably need to specify what the word "church" actually means. The New Testament was originally written in Greek and the word we translate as "church" is the Greek *ekklēsia*. This compound word comes from the two Greek words that mean "out" (*ek-*) and "to call" (*klesia*).

Many people erroneously define *ekklēsia* as "people who are called out." This way of thinking about the word may make a good point in a sermon—"the church is called out of the world"—and this teaching does appear in the New Testament (John 17:6; Rom 12:2), but it is not the word *ekklēsia* itself that tells us that we are not to conform to the world. Etymology (i.e., word origin or history) may help us understand a word's meaning, but not always. Meanings of words change over time. For example, the English word "awful" combines the two words "awe" and "full," and it originally meant "full of awe," but these days "awful" has the opposite meaning. At the time the New Testament was written, the word *ekklēsia* did not mean "called out"; it simply meant "the assembly" or "group of people." In Matthew 16, Jesus is simply saying that he will establish his group, his people.

Now we see the fulfillment of the promise Jesus made in Mathew 16 as the church is established and the community comes together in Acts 2. That early group begins to encounter difficulty very soon because they really do not know what the group they just joined is supposed to be doing. In all the teachings of Jesus, he never lined out the day-to-day workings of his church. Modern Christians may be surprised to realize that while Jesus talked a lot about the establishment of the "kingdom of God," he never detailed the practical implementation of it. We have records of hundreds of Jesus's teachings; never in those stories or parables does he lay out exactly how the church will function, nor does he give detailed instructions of the administration of his church.

It's shocking, really: Jesus established his church but gave very little or no instructions as to what this church should do. Think back on the instructions of Christ. He teaches almost entirely on our relationship with God, our relationships with other people, or the nature of the church/kingdom of God. There is almost nothing about how that church/kingdom would function in the real world after his ascension. We would have done things differently. If we had wanted to establish a group of people that would exist for thousands of years, we would have given detailed instructions on how that group should carry out its day-to-day affairs. Jesus does things differently (cf. Isa 55:8).

The church is established in Acts 2, and its members begin to function as best they can. That early group was doing the same thing we are doing today: they were attempting to discover the mission of the church. They were asking the same questions and involving themselves in the same discussions and studies that occupy us today. They were struggling to understand what it meant to be part of this assembly that belongs to Jesus. We believe that Jesus is the Son of God. Because of this belief, we have repented, been baptized, and the Lord has added us to his church. But now what? What do we do? What is the mission of the church? What am I supposed to do now that I have been added to the church?

The book of Acts chronicles the spread of the gospel and the establishment of congregations of the church of Jesus. It also gives us valuable insight to the work of the early church. Throughout the book of Acts and the epistles (letters written to the first churches), the Holy Spirit gives us clues and detailed instruction concerning the work and day-to-day activities of the early church. We can see the very earliest actions of the church in Acts 2:42–47. They ate together and prayed. They praised God, lived in peace, and they met each other's physical needs. They looked to the Apostles for direction and continued in their teachings, while having fellowship with each other.

As the early church matured, the role of the church developed. In Acts 6, we see the church growing, but a problem arose. The Grecians felt that their widows were being neglected. The church needed more organization in benevolence. The church selected men to oversee the benevolence program so that the ministry of the word would not be neglected. The apostles continued to teach and evangelize while the newly selected men oversaw this new and neglected area of work.

This passage reveals several important truths. The work of the church involved study and teaching of the word, and the church took care of its members. The text refers to these two major works as (1) ministry of the word and (2) serving tables. After the resolution of the conflict, numbers again started to increase (Acts 6:7). We should think of conflict resolution as a work of the church. Sometimes people will say, "Two of the most important works of the church are (1) saving the lost and (2) keeping the saved, saved." Much of the work of the church can fit into these two large categories, but much more is involved.

The early Christians had the apostles to help guide and teach them how each congregation should function. They wrote down their instruction, which can now guide us just as it did the first Christians. The majority of the New Testament consists of letters written to congregations, for the most part giving detailed and specific instructions on the issues each congregation faced. It is our responsibility to study those letters and to make sure that we are functioning as a group according to the instructions given to the church.

It is interesting that Jesus taught mainly about the actions of individuals and that he did not teach much about the actions of the assembly. Could it be that in many ways the church is to act like an extension of the individuals who make up the church? Jesus taught us how to be the individuals we need to be. If each of us will act the way we should and do the things we should according to his teachings, we may be surprised to find that we are fulfilling the mission of the church.

Discussion Questions

The church is referred to in the New Testament as many different things. Each comparison or metaphor carries with it certain ideas that help us see the purpose and mission of the church. For the following verses, discuss how the metaphors used help us envision the purpose and mission of the church. Think about these questions for each metaphor:

1. What is it?

2. What does it do?

3. What is its purpose?

4. What is the point of comparing it to the church?

Soldier

"No one engaged in warfare entangles himself with the affairs of *this* life, that he may please him who enlisted him as a soldier" (2 Tim 2:4, NKJV).

Flock

"Therefore take heed to yourselves and to all the flock, among which the Holy Spirit has made you overseers, to shepherd the church of God which He purchased with His own blood" (Acts 20:28).

Body

"And He Himself gave some *to be* apostles, some prophets, some evangelists, and some pastors and teachers, for the equipping of the saints for the work of ministry, for the [a]edifying of the body of Christ" (Eph 4:11–12).

Bride

"For I am jealous for you with godly jealousy. For I have betrothed you to one husband, that I may present *you as* a chaste virgin to Christ" (2 Cor 11:2).

Family/Household and Citizens/Community

"Now, therefore, you are no longer strangers and foreigners, but fellow citizens with the saints and members of the household of God" (Eph 2:19).

Church

"And I also say to you that you are Peter, and on this rock I will build My church, and the gates of Hades shall not prevail against it" (Matt 16:18).

Scripture Index

Contributors

Bill Bagents (D.Min. Amridge University) is Professor of Ministry, Counseling, and Biblical Studies at Heritage Christian University (HCU).

Jeremy Barrier (Ph.D. Brite Divinity School, Texas Christian University) is Associate Professor of Biblical Literature at HCU.

Ted Burleson (D.Min. Harding School of Theology) is a professor at Amridge University and Minister of the Hamilton Church of Christ in Hamilton, Alabama.

Jim Collins is Director of Enrollment Services at HCU.

Nathan Daily (Ph.D. in progress Claremont Graduate University) is HCU Registrar and Associate Professor of Religion.

Lori Eastep is an alumna of HCU (B.A. '04) and currently serves as the Director of Communications at Mars Hill Bible School.

Ed Gallagher (Ph.D. Hebrew Union College) is Associate Professor of Christian Scripture at HCU.

Philip Goad is an alumnus of HCU (B.A. '11) and serves as HCU Vice President for Advancement.

Travis Harmon (M.Min. Heritage Christian University) is Director of Student Services and Instructor of Ministry at HCU.

Michael Jackson (Ed.D. Union University) is Vice President for Academic Affairs and Associate Professor of Education and New Testament at HCU.

C. Wayne Kilpatrick (M.A.R. Haring School of Theology) is HCU Professor of Church History.

Brad McKinnon (M.Min Freed-Hardman University; M.A. University of North Alabama) is Associate Professor of History and Director of Field Education at HCU.

Rusty Pettus is an alumnus of HCU (B.A. '98) and serves as an academic advisor in the College of Engineering at the University of Alabama.

Printed in the USA
CPSIA information can be obtained
at www.ICGtesting.com
JSHW010246080624
64439JS00010B/182

9 781732 048324